NO ONE WANTS TO
BUY YOUR STUFF

Publisher: MI Consulting & Media
https://mirandaivey.com

ISBN: 978-0-6489334-0-3

Categories: Business, Education

NO ONE WANTS TO BUY YOUR STUFF

(How to Carve Out Your Place in a Busy Online World)

MIRANDA IVEY

DEDICATION

This book is dedicated to my dad, you taught
me more than you could ever know.

I finally finished the book we were going to write.

CONTENTS

Introduction

I t all started in 2013 with macrame. If I am being totally honest, it started with an ankle injury. I was laid up on the couch and my best friend came over. She took one look and said to me, *'You're not going to last 6 weeks doing nothing; what are you going to do?'* I blurted out, *'I want to make a macrame pot hanging. I think we could turn it into a Do-It-Yourself kit and sell them'*

Now I'd never made a macrame hanging in my life. I knew nothing about macrame. However, I'd come across this new wave of online craft businesses starting up. Doing some research (scrolling on Instagram) I'd found a group of women who had devoted fans and large social media followings. The crazy thing was, they were making a living selling objects like handmade ceramic salt and pepper shakers.

It made me think: "While they're making craft, the rest of us are keenly watching and living our craft life vicariously from the outside. I'm willing to bet I'm not the only one who would like some easy to do craft projects in my life."

Turns out I was right.

A few weeks later my first online business, Macramake, was born. I had no idea where this macrame journey was going to take me. I simply started by following an idea that excited me. I had worked as a marketer and publicist for a number of years so I knew how to sell. However much the same as everyone who pivots from having a day job to running their own business, I'd never had to promote 'me' before.

In 12 months, the same friend and I went from our first dismal market stalls in Byron Bay to making $6,000 in one weekend at a specialist craft market. We had an online store and also sold through Etsy. We used conversations with customers in "real life" to then create online marketing content. We leveraged our social media to make more sales. We grew our social media presence to thousands of followers.

After just over a year working together, with my first baby on the way, I sold my half of Macramake to my friend and business partner. The business was then sold to someone else and someone else again. Seven years later, the business still exists and has crossed three states!

Since then I've been on a wild online ride from learning the ins and outs of social media marketing to running my own social media and Facebook ads agency. For the past three years I've almost exclusively managed paid Facebook and Instagram ads; helping business owners find new audiences for their online courses and products. I've been behind the scenes for well-known entrepreneurs, spending tens of thousands of dollars to make even more in return.

During this time I've come to realise that I'm more passionate than ever about helping small business owners put their best foot forward online. Many of them who I speak with are frustrated and burnt out. They've done their study to become a therapist, a practitioner, or a coach and then they've realised... *I now have to learn marketing too?*

We all know social media has completely changed the marketing landscape. On the downside, there's no ready-made audience glued to a TV, radio, or newspaper. On the upside, the barriers are non-existent when it comes to sharing your unique business idea with the world. You can start your own page with the click of a button and you are part of the conversation!

The problem is, that there's no one there to listen when you're only just starting out.

This book is for...
- The mum who runs an online business so she can be there when the kids get home from school.
- The woman who wants to bring in her own income by sharing her passion with the world.
- The professional who has a degree and now has to 'market' themselves.
- The person who has pivoted in their business and is unsure how to translate their prior experience to what they offer now.

I've called this book *"No One Wants to Buy Your Stuff"* to help you start from the beginning. I've written it for the business owner who believes that just by creating a website the customers will come.

I'll bet that for some of you reading this, people aren't even looking for what you're selling. They're not Googling *clarity coach for mums'*, *'self-love coach'* or a *'peak performance pilates instructor'* (just a few examples of businesses I've worked with).

Once you know what you're selling, you'll have to carve out your own place in the world. The good news is you have a clean slate. There are no preconceptions as to what you have to look or sound like. In my experience, the more 'out of the box' you are, the better.

You're part of the new breed of online business owners. You can show up and start marketing whenever you choose. You decide what you want to be known for and then you get to create something out of nothing. You don't have to ask for permission from anyone.

However as you embark on your new endeavour, you'll find that there's barriers of technology. The new lingo of "growing audiences", "building brand awareness" and "increasing follower numbers" can feel overwhelming. Not to mention "hashtags" and "updating your stories". Added to this, all of it needs to be done on the busy and very public platforms of Facebook and Instagram.

The goal of this book is to make marketing enjoyable for you. To help you realise that it all comes down to how you can best share your knowledge and experience online. That as a passionate multi-talented entrepreneur, practitioner, therapist or business owner, you truly are the best person to market your business.

If you've ever wanted to stand out in a crowded market...

If you've ever wondered how others seem to be everywhere at once...

If you've ever wanted to put yourself out there in a way that feels good...

This book is for you.

By reading this book and completing the action tasks, you'll become known as a leader in your field. You'll have content ideas that connect with your target audience. You'll have a plan to help move your big ideas forward. Best of all you'll be more comfortable about being visible online than ever before.

Ready?

Let's share your fabulousness with the world!

CHAPTER 1

Start With The End In Mind

"The secret of getting ahead is getting started."

– MARK TWAIN.

I n Australia, there are new businesses starting online every day. I'll bet that there's already a lot of people who do what you do or offer something similar. Added to that, recent market research has shown that consumers are now more price-conscious than ever.

So how do you run a business when you can't or don't always want to be discounting? How do you stand out online when there are many other people offering the same services that you do? The answer is to build quality relationships.

Having quality relationships with people online will give you the opportunity to showcase your products and services, as well as the depth of your knowledge and experience.

"'Good quality' for Australians is perceived primarily in terms of the relationship they have with those around them and the organisations with which they are involved.[1]" In short, people buy from people and businesses they like.

I do this all the time. I drive past five cafes to buy coffee from the one I 'like.' I changed to a dentist that a friend recommended and now I drive 20 minutes passing several others. I went to a two-day workshop and then joined a nine month online program with a Life Coach because I trusted she could help me.

If your goal is to be able to charge a premium rate for your products and services, then you need to invest in quality relationships with your fans, followers, subscribers, video viewers and website visitors.

MARKETING IS A JOURNEY

In today's landscape, social media marketing is often how we start a relationship with people long before they purchase anything from us. Every post on social media is an opportunity to build relationships with potential customers.

Consider them to be your friends. Instead of simply yelling 'BUY MY STUFF!!!' and then becoming frustrated when no one does, it's time to start giving them many reasons to do it.

First, we need to narrow down what you're selling. Many

---

[1] IBSA Cultural Imprints at Work Report, March 2011

business owners I work with put the 'multi' in multi-passionate entrepreneurs, as they have so many skills and services to offer the world. They want to sell the cart, the horse, the stable, the hay, the water and a person to ride the horse, all in one social media post. And they wanted to sell it yesterday.

I understand that it can be hard to narrow what you do down to just one thing. Let's focus on what you want to be selling now, or in the next few months. This is why we "start with the end in mind" using my Path of Ascension method.

The Path of Ascension is a one page triangle shaped marketing plan to help get all of those ideas out of your head and into reality. It's how you will begin to move people from your social media towards purchasing your products and services.

If you've tried marketing funnels before, that's ok. This is not a funnel but a reverse funnel. My clients have told me that they think it makes more sense this way, some even tell me they love the Path of Ascension exercise.

'I've never understood funnels until you explained them this way'

- PENNY

'I love this method, it's so much more optimistic than a funnel!'

- CLARE

THE PATH OF ASCENSION

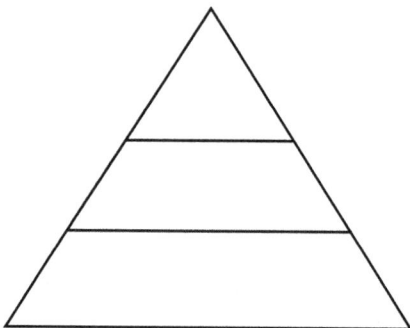

Step 1 - Draw your Triangle

Draw a triangle on a piece of paper so you understand you're leading to one point.

Then draw two lines through the triangle approximately one third and two thirds down.

You may have a million things that you want to offer the world, but for the purposes of this exercise, just choose one section/ aspect/ offer/ course from your business.

Step 2 - Write down your ultimate goal

At the top of the triangle, enter the most expensive or profitable product, service or program that you want to sell. The 'thing' that you want people to purchase right now. It may be only one aspect of your business, but it can be difficult to promote different products and services all at once.

For example, you may want to sell a package of 3 yoga sessions for $50 or 3 x psychology consultations for $499. You might have an online program you're selling for $997 or you may be offering up places on your exclusive Mastermind retreat that cost $10,000 each. No matter what it is, start by putting what you want to sell in the top section of the triangle.

Now we have a goal.

Step 3 - Brainstorm your marketing opportunities

Go to the wide section at the bottom of the triangle. This is where you'll put in your 'free social media marketing' content. You don't need to come up with specific topic ideas at this point, they will come later. Simply write down how you currently communicate with potential clients through social and online media.

Your list may include:
- Facebook posts and videos
- Instagram posts and stories
- Email newsletters
- YouTube videos
- Blogs
- Podcasts
- Posting in Facebook groups

Brainstorm as many ideas you can about many ways you have to interact with people online. Focus on what you enjoy doing first, then add in a few that may be a stretch for you. For example, you may love creating Facebook posts but have an aversion to doing video. Write that down as it's a marketing tool you have available to you.

Doing this exercise may also reveal marketing tactics you're not currently taking advantage of. (Maybe it's time to say hello to your email list that hasn't heard from you since last year!)

It's the content for this bottom section that we'll be focussing on for most of this book; specifically how you can use all your free or low-cost marketing opportunities to drive people up your Path of Ascension.

While 'free marketing' is awesome, without an end goal all that time and effort making gorgeous Instagram posts may not make you any money.

Step 4 - The bridging step

This middle section of the triangle is your bridging step between social media clicks and paying customers. It's often called a lead magnet and it involves a commitment between your potential customers and your business. Usually, you deliver free information or solve a problem they're having in return for their email address (and ability to market to them in their inbox.)

For me, this book is in the middle section of the triangle. It's an opportunity for you, my readers, to get to know me for a low cost. By reading my book you'll realise that I 'know my stuff' about online marketing. If you also like how I share this knowledge, there's a chance you may start to trust me. Then you may even move up the triangle to purchase one of my marketing programs.

Consider it this way, if I simply asked you to pay $997 for a marketing program straight from one social media post, it probably won't work, would it?

Your job right now is to simply consider the middle section of the triangle. If you have a free opt-in available on your website write down what this is in your middle section. As you move through this book, I want you to consider whether it's still 'right' for taking your potential customers on a journey to purchasing.

If you don't have an opt-in or a middle step currently, here are a few ideas for you:

- A free opt-in[2], that moves potential clients from knowing they have a few "symptoms" to understanding that they have a "problem" that needs to be solved
- A free strategy call, that allows you to assess their issues and offer a solution. This works well for businesses that offer a service
- A discount on your products or services to help people make their decision faster

---

[2] More on the right free opt-in in Chapter 6.

Trust Takes Time

If you've heard of the marketing phrase 'Know, Like and Trust' factor, consider the bottom section of your triangle to be 'Know' for your potential customers. Your marketing communication helps them to get to know you and what you stand for.

In the middle section, they move up to 'Like'. They like you enough to share their email address for ongoing communication (a free opt-in), their time (a discovery call), or money (discount on your products or special offer).

Over time, these potential customers will move up to the top of the triangle to 'Trust.' They trust you and show this by investing in you by making a purchase.

Now that you have done your Path of Ascension you have the start of a marketing plan. I created this method to help people realise that most of your fans and followers simply won't make the leap from the bottom of the triangle to the top in one social media post. If you've ever wondered why no one bought a place on your $10,000 Mastermind retreat from one social post or paid ad, now you know!

SUMMARY

Start on your Path of Ascension now. If you have different online products or services that you want to sell, repeat the Path of Ascension for each one. Unless you have sophisticated marketing strategies it can be very hard to sell different products and services all at once.

If you're just getting started, I would suggest focussing on one product or service at the top of your triangle and repeating the process as required.

Take Action Now

- Draw your Path of Ascension Triangle on paper
- Decide what you want to offer and place it at the top of the Path of Ascension
- Write down all the 'channels' you have available for building relationships in the bottom section
- Consider your middle section or 'bridging step'. If you're unsure, this will be covered in Chapter 6.

CHAPTER 2

Sell With Feeling

"When there is no love, there is no understanding"

- OSCAR WILDE

When I was a kid my dad and I played the game where something was hidden and he directed me to find it by calling out 'cold... colder' As I moved closer he said 'warm... hot... burning hot' until bingo! I found it.

In online marketing, the same concept applies. Those people who've never heard of you are called 'cold audiences'. As they move towards getting to know you and trusting you, they're warm audiences. By the time they're ready to buy, they're burning hot!

When you're starting out with social media for your business, you only need one strategy in mind. Focus on how you want people to feel as a result of working with you and buying your products. This will turn them into customers faster.

HOW DO YOU WANT PEOPLE TO FEEL?

By now, you have an idea of what you'll ultimately be selling to people. At the bottom of the triangle is where you'll start to make them understand who you are, what you stand for and why they *should* be doing business with you.

But what's the *feeling* you want them to have as a result of doing business with you?

When I joined my business partner Angela at Dotti Media, we weren't sure of this feeling. We thought it was more about showing the world how smart we were. As a fresh new business, we always felt like we had to prove ourselves in some way. Even though we were interested in high-level marketing strategies and thought by sharing this content it would show how clever we were. However the content that interested us wasn't what interested our audience.

What this meant for our social media content was that our carefully thought out posts got low engagement as it wasn't what people wanted. When your posts receive low engagement, this in turn will lower your reach on Facebook and Instagram.

In contrast, our presentations at in person workshops were an entirely different matter. We were known as being able to break down complex concepts into easily understood steps, while also helping people understand they could have fun with marketing. We left people feeling empowered to take control of their marketing and not feel as though it was beyond them. I didn't realise at the time that it would have served us better to involve this side of us into our social media marketing.

After three years in business, Angela and I parted ways at the end of 2017. In my half of the business break up, I received ownership of all our social channels, mailing list and website. Running the business on my own, I often claimed I was *too busy* to post on social media or email my subscribers. To be honest, I wasn't clear how I wanted to make people feel when they did business with me. Seeing as I was "busy enough", I didn't value the importance of keeping in touch and building trust.

PEOPLE BUY RESULTS NOT PRODUCTS

In 2019 I wanted to pivot in my business. My goal (top of the triangle) was to transition out of working full time as a Facebook ads Manager and offer a coaching program. This was a new direction for me and what I had previously been known for. Using social media was an opportunity for me to test my messaging and see what my audience resonated with. It was time I started showing up.

I began to post regular videos on Facebook. I allowed myself to express my opinions and views on marketing. I began to uncover how I wanted to make people feel. Some of you may know already how you want people to feel after working with you. For me, it took a process of evolving ideas and receiving feedback from others with the content I shared.

By being my most fabulous self, whether it's talking into a banana on rollerskates, or simply hitting record on a video where I'm not 'perfect' (I rarely wear make-up) I hope that it will help others see that their most crazy, not-normal self is welcome.

As I said in Chapter 1, people do business with people they like. People also don't simply buy a product or a service, they buy how it makes them *feel*. For example, if you're selling an online program on self-care, your customers aren't buying your videos and worksheets. They're buying the results once they've invested in themselves and done the activities you've created.

Take a moment, look up from this page and ask yourself:

How do you want your clients and customers to feel after working with you?

Write this at the top of your triangle to keep it top of mind.

WHY SHOULD SOMEONE LIKE YOUR PAGE?

I remember the first time I posed this question at a social media workshop in Adelaide, '*So why should anyone like your page?*' You could have heard a pin drop. No one had ever thought about why someone, other than their friends and family, would be interested in what's happening on their Facebook page.

As business owners, artists and practitioners, they all knew that they *should* be on Facebook so they jumped in and set up their page. They know they *should* be promoting themselves so they posted product photos or promoting blogs. They shared videos that they found funny because they knew they *should* post regularly.

Despite all this posting, they had never thought why anyone *should* follow them. Nor had they considered how their non-stop promotional posts might not be all that engaging for potential clients.

SO WHY SHOULD ANYONE LIKE YOU? AND WHY DOES IT MATTER?

Your social media pages are often the first point of call for potential customers as they decide whether to buy from you or the 39 other people who sell similar 'stuff'.

The Yellow Social Media Report Australia 2018 confirms this: *"One in three (potential customers) say they will inspect a brand's social media presence before making an online purchase if they have not purchased from their website before."*

What this means: If you have 73 likes on your Facebook page and you're only posting funny cat memes, or you haven't posted since June 2019, the person who is deciding about whether to buy from you online may look somewhere else. Building your social media following is important in an online world.

CONTROVERSY REWARDS WITH ENGAGEMENT

Every time you post on Facebook or Instagram, the algorithm is monitoring how quickly people like, click, comment and share your posts. Put simply if people engage with your posts, then even more people will see them. If you have a Facebook page and you've seen the 'Reach' metric and wondered why only 126 people saw your post when you have 523 page likes, then this is why.

The way to work with the algorithm so that your content (that you've worked so hard on!) can reach more people is to post content that is engaging. Engaging content speaks the language of your audience while coming also positioning you in a place of leadership.

Constance Hall (@constancehall) is loud, proud and incredibly polarising. Her fans respect her for this because she's able to put into words what they are already thinking of themselves. She's gone from mum blogger to social media superstar. She has created her own successful fashion label and mobilises her 'army of queens' (her fans) to help her support charitable causes.

By standing out and having an opinion you will set yourself apart from others in your industry. Embrace your uniqueness and own it.

Here's a few more examples where standing out was rewarded with engagement:

- Bronnie Ware (@bronnieware) wrote a blog post on "The Top 5 Regrets of the Dying" about her conversations with palliative care patients. It challenged how people viewed their lives. This one post went so viral that it was turned into a multi-million copy bestseller translated into multiple languages.
- A post by Rachel Hume, a naturopath (@niyama_naturopathic), who went against the status quo and called out intermittent fasting as 'not working' gained traction, both for and against. This resulted in huge engagement on her page.

- The Wine Traveller (@the_wine_traveller) discovered that their unique voice was knowing the difference between organic and most other wine purchased in bottle shops. By continually sharing information on this topic, they were able to showcase not just their knowledge but also gain a legion of new customers.

I can imagine many people reading this now are thinking, *"You don't know my audience. They would be turned away by this."* Or you may also be thinking, *"I don't want to attract haters."*

If you're more worried about haters than the people who will love what you're doing and who need to hear your voice... then toe the line, sound like everyone else in your industry and see how long it takes you to build a following.

BE DIFFERENT

To stand out in a busy online world, it's time to stop being the bland vanilla version of who you think you're meant to be, sound or look like. It's your point of difference that will make you stand out from the crowd and attract customers who love you for you.

No more sitting on the fence and not having an opinion about what's happening in your industry. People want to know the real you. Ultimately it will be how you express yourself online that will help them determine whether they want to buy from you or not.

You can do this by brainstorming 10 - 20 commonly held

beliefs or misconceptions about what you do or your industry. It's your time to prove others wrong or uphold beliefs if you believe they're right. To find what commonly held beliefs there are about your industry, engage your potential customers in conversation.

If you're in Facebook groups of similar people, use the search tool to see what people are saying about what you do. The more you can speak with your customers or potential customers, the better you will become at writing social media content about what problems they're having.

What are commonly held beliefs about what you're selling?

Example: An online marketer
1. You have to follow the steps from famous marketing gurus or you'll never make any money online.
2. You need a podcast, a professionally designed logo and a website before you begin.
3. You need to have the right look.
4. You need to have a big budget in order to run Facebook ads.
5. When you do run Facebook ads they're confusing, don't work, and cost lots of money.
6. Everyone else is selling the same thing as me, so why bother.
7. If you don't have a big email list you can't sell online.
8. If you're not an expert in your niche, no one will buy from you.

9. I don't have the right experience to sell.
10. Marketing is confusing so why even bother.

Example: For a home-based online Pilates instructor
1. You have to be fit to do Pilates.
2. You have to be flexible.
3. You need fancy equipment.
4. It's the same as yoga.
5. I can learn for free from YouTube videos.
6. It won't work for me as I have injuries.
7. It won't work for me as I have a health condition.
8. I'm not very good at relaxing.
9. I don't think I can learn online.
10. I'm doing other exercise, I don't think I can fit this in.

Each of these is a great topic to answer in your social media posts. Leverage your experience and create more content by stretching out these ideas. You don't need to solve world peace in one post. Challenge one belief = one post only.

SUMMARY

Stop holding yourself back from posting what you want. Start the conversations online that you know you want to have, that your clients need to hear. When it comes to people buying your stuff, having an opinion will help you stand out in between the other businesses in your industry. Take small steps towards expressing yourself on a regular basis and being more 'you'. Watch as your true fanbase begins to grow.

Take Action Now

Have a look at some of the accounts that you admire and have large followings (you have my permission to scroll!)

- What is it about them that makes you want to read and engage with their posts?
- What do their fans say about them?
- If you've been posting content on your page, go back and read it. Do you think that you're giving your fans the real you?
- If people are commenting, what do they say?
- What would you like your fans to say under your posts?
- Are you having the conversations online that you want to have?
- Why should people follow your page?
- How do you want them to feel after they purchase from you?
- Go back to that list of 10 - 20 commonly held beliefs about your industry, and get creative about how you can share your opinion about one of these through a video, image post or just text.

CHAPTER 3

Your Niche Within A Niche

"Invisible threads are the strongest ties."

- NIETZCHE

By now you're clear on what you're selling. You're beginning to voice your opinion out there in the online world. You know how you want to make people feel. Now it's time to find your people.

Spoiler alert; It's not everyone.

You may have heard of the concept of 'niching.' That is where you choose to sell a particular product to a particular group of people.

Niche - definition by UrbanDictionary.com

1. A position or activity that particularly suits somebody's talents and personality or that somebody can make his or her own.

2. An area of the market specialising in one type of product or service.

But wait... what if you want to help *everyone*... or even *every woman*?

You still can! The beauty of niching is that while your content becomes more specific, you are still able to work with everyone. The power in tailoring your messaging is that your niche market will understand that you are the person for them.

This is what will help you become an authority in your niche.

NICHING HELPS YOU CONNECT

Recently I set up a paid Facebook advertising campaign for a free online webinar. I wrote the ads as I normally would but it didn't feel right. I was calling people 'business owners' and it simply seemed too general to hit the mark.

Straightaway the link click costs were high. This meant that the ads weren't engaging people enough to even bother clicking on them in their Facebook newsfeeds. Seeing as, I wanted people to register for the webinar, this was going to be the first thing they had to do.

I made the decision to change my ad copy. I tailored it to speak directly to health professionals and the specific problems they had with having their Facebook ads approved. After this change, my lead costs for the training registrations dropped dramatically, from $8 to $4 per registration. I think you'll agree that getting double the amount of registrations for the same price is a good idea!

The content for my webinar didn't change nor did what I was selling. However, by tailoring my social media messaging to a niche group, I was more visible to the people who I wanted to target.

If you have been feeling frustrated in the past with the results of your marketing, this may be an opportunity to rethink *who* you've been marketing to. While I wish everything would work immediately, failure can be a catalyst for the change you desire. By tuning in to what's not working, you might find a whole new audience who wants to buy your stuff.

HOW TO FIND YOUR NICHE

I'm sure that using niching to direct your marketing sounds like a great idea... until you don't know who your niche market is. I have a simple way around this that I used to completely change my marketing and business. In turn, I went on to create a successful online coaching program and was invited to speak at a national conference for my specific niche.

Rewind to late 2018. My son was born in June and I was on government subsidised maternity leave. In the past year, my business partner and I had decided to go our separate ways, I became pregnant and was burnt out being a Facebook ads Manager. Mainly because I was working across a wide variety of industries from selling e-commerce to high-end coaching.

While ads management had been lucrative, I knew that the role needed a lot of my time. Each new niche required me to understand how their audience spoke and what they would respond to. This certainly wasn't going to be sustainable with two small children under 3 running around. I used the break that my maternity leave gave me to consider how I wanted to run my business and who I wanted to work with.

I asked myself three questions:
- Who had been my favourite clients over the past four years?
- Why had they been my favourite clients?
- What results had I delivered for them?

My answer was my clients in the health and wellness niche.

I enjoyed the clients, they were easy to work with and I thought highly of the programs and services they offered. So without asking anyone's opinion, I decided this would be my niche. (As I said above, I still could work with people in other industries, I simply tailored my social media marketing more towards this market.)

My next step was to start becoming known in this particular niche. In order to do this, I called a Naturopath friend and asked if I could set up and run some Facebook ad campaigns for her as long as I could record myself and create a training program. To generate interest and sales, I ran a free live webinar that was specific to the industry on 'How to have your Health and Wellness Facebook ads approved faster'.

After this I became known in the 'naturopathic industry' as the go-to Facebook ads specialist. I was introduced to Tammy Guest who mentors Naturopaths. A special training session for Tammy's group followed and then she invited me to be a guest speaker at her NatEx conference in early 2020.

I never asked anyone if I could niche down to the health and wellness industry. I didn't have to do this, but what followed meant I made a name for myself. I did have some experience but as I wanted more I offered my services to someone for free to help both our businesses grow.

As a result, my business was successful and worked for me in the time I had available. I also became known as the go-to person in this niche. You may already have an idea of who your niche is. If not, complete the questions at the end of this chapter to discover who to work with.

WHAT IS A NICHE WITHIN A NICHE?

Most of the time, people I speak to know that their ideal clients or niche are men or women of a particular age group. Some of them have completed an Ideal Customer Avatar exercise or similar. Ideal customer exercises usually involve answering a number of questions about who the ideal client is, age, occupation, how many children, what they eat for breakfast, what clothing labels they wear... the list goes on.

The trouble I've found with this exercise is your niche is categorised by demographics. It's broad brush strokes and your target market may not always fit nicely into a specific demographic box. By taking this a step further to uncover their psychographics, you'll start to get inside their heads. You'll understand where your target niche is at in their life. More importantly, know what problems they're having and what they want.

Psychographic - definition by Urbandictionary.com
   The study and classification of people according to their attitudes, aspirations, and other psychological criteria, especially in market research.

Understanding your customer's attitudes and aspirations will assist in directing your marketing. In turn, this makes it easier to create products to match and guide your copywriting for ads and sales pages.

BEYOND AN IDEAL CUSTOMER AVATAR EXERCISE

Let's say you're part of the new breed of online entrepreneurs. You solve a problem that keeps your target audience up at night but who doesn't know how to 'google it' to find the answer.

An example of this is a Personal Trainer Coach. That means, a Coach for Personal Trainers who want to grow their business. No one is googling this, they may not even know where to start. Enter social media messaging and paid ads that are specific to her niche.

In order for this Coach to be seen and successful, she needs to speak to where these personal trainers are at and what they're going through. She can then position herself as the person who understands their problems and take them where they want to go in business.

If she was to complete a normal Ideal Customer Avatar exercise, the questions are often framed like this.

Is your Ideal Customer...
- Male or female?
- Age?
- Children or no children?
- What do they watch on television?
- Who do they follow on social media?
- What do they like doing on the weekend?

My ideal customer is... Female, personal trainer, aged 20 - 45, two kids, working part-time, likes watching Survivor and follows Michelle Bridges and Kayla Itsines on social media.

This works well except it doesn't allow you to drill deeper into why your niche is really having the problems that will see them seek help.

Following on from this, here are some extra psychographic questions. We know that this Ideal Customer is a personal trainer, but we need to drill down further.

Where is this woman in her life?
She's at a point in her life where she wants to make running her own business a success. She feels like she's tried everything she can and wants to take it further.

How long has she been in business?
1 - 2 years.

Is she just starting out or looking to grow?

She's looking to grow, or if she's just starting out, she already has a good base point.

Why is she seeking help?

She knows that there must be an easier way to grow her business. She's seen other trainers do it and doesn't know what that vital missing point is.

Is she burnt out being a mum and running a business?

She is a mum but she's doing ok.

Is she transitioning from working at a gym and into her own boss?

Yes, she wants to make more money than just an hourly wage but she doesn't know how to do it.

Even a few short questions we're building up a targeted picture of who the client is and where she's at. These questions are vital if you want your posts, your ad copy and your sales pages to leap out of the screen because your customers are thinking *'How can this person read my mind? I really need to buy their stuff!'*

The more you can pinpoint what your customers are going through, the more you will be able to create content that connects. Even if you know your niche, drill down further using the questions at the end of this chapter. Then you will find your niche within a niche.

WHY YOU CAN STILL WORK WITH EVERYONE

The biggest fear most people have when they niche down is that they will miss out on making money. I've been told so many times that if *'I cater to just one group such as mums, I will offend all the non-mums.'* Or *'If I only cater to women, what about the men who are my clients?'*

The good news is that you can still work with everyone, but your marketing will be tailored and specific for your niche. Remember, your marketing doesn't have to be like this forever, you can change it to target a specific niche a month.

Think of a gym. They offer some classes that cater to everyone and others that are specifically for 'mums and bubs'. They put out a timetable so that mums aren't turning up with their kids to a regular class where clients are there to do a hard workout. Then those without kids (or those who just don't bring them to the gym) aren't arriving at the mums and bubs classes, which may be a bit more disruptive than regular classes.

Notice that the gym still caters to different niches. In their case, their marketing is their timetable that lets everyone know where they're meant to be.

SUMMARY

The more targeted or niche you can become, the more the right people will hear what you have to say. Even if you've always been trying to appeal to everyone, you can start niching down today.

Your goal is to find out exactly where your target audience is in their life and what they're going through. This will give you an idea about what to write in your social media marketing and may even lead to the creation of new offers, products, or services.

Take Action Now:

Determine your Niche. If you don't have one, use these questions to work out who to work with:
- Who have been your favourite clients?
- Why have they been my favourite clients?
- What results have you delivered for them?

Use these questions to discover your Niche within a Niche:
- Which niche do you work with?
- Where are they at in their lives?
- What's been a recent pivotal moment in their lives that has led them to seek help?

- What are they currently doing that they could be doing better?
- How will they know you're the person for them?
- Are there particular times of the year that they need your help? Why / why not?

BONUS IDEAS

Head to https://mirandaivey.com/expert and sign up for my 7 Day Expert Posting Challenge. You'll receive a week of post ideas and prompts for showing up as your fabulous self.

CHAPTER 4

Become An Authority (Even If You Don't Think You Are)

"I am not afraid... I was born to do this."

— JOAN OF ARC

U nless you're a tech start-up or product inventor, there are most likely plenty of other people who sell the same or similar products and services as you. To stand out from the crowd and have a thriving online business, it's time to step up and become so visible that the competition is rendered invisible. It's time to become the authority you're meant to be.

How do you become the authority on a particular topic? Show up and talk about it all the time in a myriad of different ways!

This can be daunting at first. Over time being an authority figure will become easier. Once you're clear on your niche and wanting to step into this position of authority, I encourage you to start making small positive changes. Alter your Instagram account bio. Update the About page on your website. Make videos on your topic. This truly is how you start to shine.

WHY BEING AN AUTHORITY MATTERS

When you're posting on social media, you're being placed in the Facebook and Instagram newsfeeds. That means you're competing to be seen between status updates, group updates, other pages' posts, paid ads, suggested content and more.

Facebook says that the average user has over 100,000 pieces of information that could be shown to them every day in the newsfeed. That's why in 2011 Facebook introduced Edgerank or as it's most often referred to as, the Facebook algorithm. In 2020 this highly developed artificial intelligence software determines what you see and why. Essentially Facebook has designed the algorithm to keep people scrolling, longer. That way we see more ads!

A similar algorithm has been in place on Instagram since 2016 to show you content that has received high engagement, accounts you interact with regularly, and paid ads. This is why even if you follow an account or like a business' page, you may never see their posts in your feed.

As a business on Facebook and Instagram you need to realise that:

1. It's very busy.
2. It's discouraging if no one likes your posts (and doesn't buy your stuff!)

3. It's time to start using your authority to your advantage.

If someone is scrolling through these platforms they are deciding very quickly what they are going to look at for longer than a glance. Therefore you need to jump out of the screen and demand their attention.

This can be done by creating content that connects with others while establishing your position of authority. You can do this by weaving in your years of experience, professional highlights and unique views on your industry.

SPECIALISE INSTEAD OF GENERALISE

You most likely have a title relating to your qualifications such as 'Bookkeeper' or a self-imposed title like 'Numbers Ninja.' I don't mind what you call yourself, it's more about what others know about you that will build authority.

Think about the online marketplace, where you're competing to be known in your industry and attract customers. With so many people offering similar services, do you really want to be another 'Bookkeeper?' Or do you want to get specific and tie your title in with your niche or area of interest?

What about calling yourself a 'Numbersmith for Creatives'? (An actual title of a bookkeeper I know) Or the 'Surfers Bookkeeper'?

Which do you think is easier?

-   Becoming known in the industry.

- Being recommended by others.[3]
- Standing out from the crowd.
- Coming up with social media content.

However, it is important to know that if you want to change up how your business is run or it's time to charge more, then you'll need to attract a new breed of clients. Word of mouth may not cut it any longer. This book is all about carving out your own place online to generate new enquiries and recommendations.

The good news is that you've already done the hard work in the previous chapters by deciding on your niche. By making it real you're going to feel confident in sharing this everywhere.

Grab your pen and paper and complete the following statement:

I am the go-to [insert your title] for [insert your target market].

My example: I am the go-to Marketing and Business Coach for coaches, therapists and practitioners.

Now breathe out. Look at what you've written. This is your first step to becoming an authority in your chosen niche. Start sharing this everywhere!

---

[3] Word of mouth recommendations is still a huge part of marketing even in the online world. When you specialise and share this across your social media platforms, people will have no trouble recommending you because they know who you work best with.

YOU ARE ALREADY A LEADER

These days you can become a leader in just about anything (Insta-celebrities are proof of this!) Your leadership is in how you share what you've been through, your real life experience and how you've practically applied what you know. Even if it feels shaky to begin with, it will start to become real. And once you believe it, others will too.

I can imagine the inner thoughts of new online entrepreneurs who just read the previous paragraph...

'But so and so is the authority on the subject, I can't possibly be'

'But I need XYZ qualifications to be an authority'

'I don't have enough followers/ I haven't written a book / I'm just starting out so I couldn't possibly say...'

I'm not advocating that you go around calling yourself a doctor without a degree. However, I am saying that you can choose, right now, to be a leader in your chosen field. At the start of this chapter you wrote 'I am the go-to authority on...'

Everything you've done before can assist in elevating your status in the minds of others; it's all in how you tell your story. This is the fundamental reason why people will start to listen to you and then buy your stuff.

Most people only ever share their authority on their website's About page.

41

I want you to start owning it and sharing it everywhere:

Social media posts - sharing why you are an authority, relying on those reasons why

Case studies - Use real life examples of problems people were having and how you helped them be overcome. If you're in an industry where you can't use names, generalise e.g. *'A woman recently came to me...'*

Testimonials - Testimonials are great for your website. They're even better as screenshots and shared on your social media!

Sales pages - If you're selling anything, you definitely need to use testimonials or case studies on your sales page to help drive sales

Paid Facebook & Instagram ads - An excellent use of testimonials is in paid ads, you're getting others to do your selling for you!

SUMMARY

In the same way, you must be clear about what you're selling and who you're selling it to, you also need to know why people should buy it from you. The more that you come from a position of leadership, the more people will hear it, read it and believe it. Start by identifying your new title and then share this everywhere online.

Take Action Now:

Write down your answers to:

I am the go-to [insert your title] for [insert your target market].

Think about yourself and your experience. What do you have that people will notice if you talk about yourself? Come up with 50 reasons why people 'should' do business with you. Is it your:

- Years of experience
- Life experience
- The particular niche that you've had great results in
- How many people you've worked with
- Whether you've worked with any big names

If you're not sure, ask a friend or colleague why they would do business with you. What is it about your story that makes people listen?

Then start to weave this into everywhere!

CHAPTER 5

Get Out Of Your (Video) Comfort Zone

"Whatever you can do, or dream you can, begin it. Boldness has genius, magic, and power in it. Begin it now"

— GOETHE

One of the online entrepreneurs I know turns up more than anyone else. She writes a blog regularly, sends a newsletter out to her email list weekly, creates video content and puts out a weekly podcast. She's very savvy in understanding her niche and creating programs that serve her clients at different points in their journey. Is it any wonder that her revenue doubles every year?

Marketing is the process of saying the same thing over and over again until you strike on the way that resonates with people the best. A singer doesn't expect to just jump on stage and start singing perfectly in front of an audience for the first time. She spends hours and hours rehearsing her songs, practicing different ways of doing it. She stumbles over certain words until she finds her groove.

Your marketing is no different. Chances are, you will suck to begin with. Especially when it comes to something like making a video if you've never done it before. The goal is to not get frustrated but to enjoy the process, even if no one is watching.

If you've been complaining that no one wants to buy your stuff, then sooner or later you'll need to start putting yourself out there. We may as well start now.

MARKETING IS NOT ABOUT YOU

One of the most common complaints I hear about creating videos for Facebook and Instagram is that it's difficult. One has to have the perfect background, makeup on, hair brushed, editing software... Or are these simply excuses? Is it more that you're worried if people will think that your video isn't very good? Or you don't have anything to say?

I used to spend ages creating the right background for my videos, moving plants around or standing in front of a pretty picture. I'd often spend longer arranging items to go behind me than I would in front of the camera. I'd put on lipstick, find a shirt to wear (because I thought this made me look professional) and then try to sound formal and smart.

I came across as an uninteresting wooden stick who talked about Facebook ads.

45

In order to get over my nerves, I set myself a challenge of a weekly video. My thought process was; *'I want to start sucking at this. I want to look back in a few months and see how far I've come'.* You know those people who you admire online, who seem so natural on video? They sucked at first too.

I know that it can be scary having a video camera or phone in your face, but the best thing about video is that fans, followers and potential clients can hear you, see you and start to get to know you - fast. If the idea of making the perfect image or writing an epic blog post has been holding you back, hitting record on your phone is an excellent way to get your marketing 'done'.

BATCH YOUR VIDEOS

One of my favourite aspects of using video in online marketing is that it can be batched easily. Simply brainstorm a number of topics, set your phone up and hit record. If you've got a tripod, great, use it. If not an open laptop can work or a pot plant or some books. I often suggest to my clients to get outside of the office and into the fresh air too. Natural light makes everyone look good!

If you're worried about adding in too many 'umms' or doing something weird with your mouth while you speak, here are a few ways to get started.

- Speak to the camera just like you're speaking to a friend or your mum. Try to forget it's even there
- Record video just for you, and yes, play it back and watch

it carefully. What would you change? Please don't be too critical of yourself!

- Set up a group on Facebook, don't invite anyone to join, and do Facebook lives just for you.
- If you're using your phone, look at the camera (that dot above the screen) because if you're looking at you, you won't be looking at the camera.
- Use the content topics at the end of this chapter to brainstorm ideas prior to hitting record.
- Record 4 - 5 videos all at once and publish them for a month on Facebook and Instagram.

As someone who has recorded and uploaded videos with lettuce in my teeth and washing drying in the background, I can tell you, starting is as simple as pressing a button. Best of all, you don't like the video you've recorded, press delete and they're gone.

REPURPOSE YOUR VIDEO

It can be difficult to keep sharing the same message over and over again, especially when you only want to say "buy my stuff/ book my service / pay me for a consultation". And yet, in the repetition, you'll start to be known for what you do and build your reputation as an authority on the subject.

However, if you're putting all this effort into creating an amazing (or moderately adequate) video only to post it once on Facebook, have it seen by 145 people and never to be used again, you're wasting your time. This is where you can use repurposing to your advantage to amplify your content across multiple channels.

Fact: No one will get angry if you repurpose your content across multiple social channels by doing it in different ways.

Also a fact: No one is checking up on you to see if you do this.

Online marketing is the never-ending piece of string that needs to be coiled. It can feel as though you're always behind. That's where choosing one particular piece of content to be your "linchpin" to repurpose can help.

Linchpin - definition by UrbanDicionary.com

A person or thing vital to an enterprise or organisation.

A *linchpin* helps you find your focus when you're over-whelmed by indecision. If you know that you've got to do this one task, I guarantee that once you've ticked that off for the week, you will find yourself feeling happier with your marketing.

Since 2019, a video has been the "linchpin" in my marketing. It's my non-negotiable done every week. Once I know that my video is uploaded, I can feel good that I've covered off the minimum in my marketing.

Here's how I make one video (approximately 2 - 5 minutes long) and share it across multiple platforms in one week.

1. Record a video and share on Facebook
2. Use this video as a topic for my weekly email newsletter with a link to Facebook to watch the video
3. Either share a short part of the video or create an image on Instagram. Tell people to watch they can watch the video on Facebook. Add a link in your Instagram bio*
4. I then use the email newsletter text or a transcription for a blog post. I upload and embed the video from Facebook or upload to YouTube.

SUMMARY

Video is a great way to connect with audiences online as they can hear you and see you. The confidence you think you need to get started will come with time. Your first video won't be a masterpiece, but your 56th might! Brainstorm ideas for topics before you jump in front of the camera so you can batch record multiple videos at once.

Take Action Now

Start brainstorming and then batch your videos with some of these content ideas:

1. How can you find out about [you have this problem]
2. How to do [insert skill]...
3. Why you would want to do it my way...
4. People often ask me...
5. People always ask me...
6. One thing I got asked this week...
7. A common thing I hear from [insert target market] is...
8. A common misconception about [area of expertise] is...

Find some natural light, set up your camera and hit record!

What is your weekly marketing "linchpin"?

CHAPTER 6

Turn Problems Into Solutions

"Each morning we are born again.
What we do today is what matters most."

- BUDDHA

H ave you ever been scrolling through Facebook only to come across a sponsored post (this is a paid ad) that is exactly what you didn't know you were looking for? This is the Facebook algorithm combined with good copywriting at work.

Facebook is tracking everything we do both on and off the site. Many websites have the Facebook tracking pixel installed in order to be able to retarget their website visitors with paid ads. As a user, this pixel sends data back to Facebook about what we're interested in, what kind of content we interact with and so much more.

As a marketer, you can use this to your advantage. Paid Facebook advertising allows you to target people based on their demographics and interests. When you're looking to find new customers, this allows you to show up on their Facebook and Instagram newsfeeds.

TELL MORE STORIES

Australians love stories. Everyone loves stories. We love to know why something exists. We love to know about the person who created it. It's the entire message of this book. If no one is buying your stuff, then you aren't telling enough stories about why they should!

Over the years some of my highest performing Facebook ads have simply been stories. They haven't been overly salesy, the focus has definitely been on people overcoming problems and offering the solution for others to find out about.

Write in a way that shows that you understand exactly the problems your customers are having in their life, weaving in specific references to the 'problem' and use the language they would use to describe it. Your post will then offer a solution, positioning you as an authority.

One of my clients runs a meditation membership site. What she 'sells' is the opportunity of inner peace. Her niche is an older woman who has been through life's challenges and found themselves often feeling worn out and unworthy. Sometimes, they've never tried meditation before or they think it involves sitting with their legs crossed for a long time which they find uncomfortable.

If someone has never experienced meditation, how will they know what she sells is for them?

By talking about the problems that they may be having. By weaving in the stories of women who are just like them. This might be my client who overcame her own obstacles to meditation and inner peace or existing members of her membership.

Problems the target audience is having:
- Feeling anxious
- Feeling that they are unworthy
- Not feeling like they're living the life they want
- Feeling lonely
- Meditation is hard work

Solutions she offers:
- Meditation can help calm anxiety
- True worth comes from within, meditation can assist with this
- Quieting the mind through meditation can help you find what you want in life
- Opportunity to connect with others as part of the membership
- Meditation can be done lying down in the comfort of your own home

All of a sudden you're no longer selling videos or meditation sessions.

TAP INTO THEIR DESIRES

Having worked in social media marketing for over 6 years, I know that there's a market for everything. Healthy lunchbox e-book? You got it! Overcoming Self Sabotage self-paced course? No doubt about it!

The secret to the businesses that are successful is that they know which niche they serve and post content that connects with them. They also understand the problems their customers are having and are actively creating offers that offer a solution.

On social media, the customers who you're aiming to attract may not even consciously be aware of the problem that you want to solve. You need to be active in helping them articulate what problems they're having.

People often struggle with this exercise but it's worth doing and even repeating on a regular basis.

Write down the answer to these questions:
- *What problem do you solve for people?*
- *What dream are you tapping into?*
- *How do you solve their problem/fulfill their dream?*

For example, I help **new online entrepreneurs** to understand **social media marketing** with my book *No One Wants to Buy Your Stuff.*

Your turn:

I help **[my target market or niche]** to **[problem they're having]** with **[your solution]**.

The clearer you are on this, the clearer your marketing will become. Now it's time to get their attention.

Example: Telling a story to promote a lead magnet opt-in. Using Authority + Niching to promote a lead magnet.

Robyn wants to become the go-to authority for busy women to eat food that helps them lose weight

What she sells:
Smoothie recipe ebook

Niche she sells it to:
Busy women

Niche within the niche:
Busy women who want to lose weight in a healthy way and don't have time for fancy ingredients.

Who she is:
Robyn is completing her Nutritionist qualification. She's 35 and feels discouraged because she's starting from scratch and has no industry experience. She doesn't feel like she could call herself an authority.

Before studying Robyn worked in corporate for 10 years.

During that time she thought she was doing everything right to lose weight from calorie counting to special diets. It turns out there was more going on inside her body than she realised, which is why she transitioned into becoming a Nutritionist. Being a Nutritionist has helped her discover more about food than she ever imagined.

Instead of some predictable copy such as:

"I'm a Nutritionist and I love smoothies! I created my smoothie book to help busy women eat breakfast on the run!"

Robyn can use her story to position herself as an authority and stand out in the newsfeed:

"I worked in a corporate job for over 10 years and thought I was doing all the right things to keep my weight under control, from special meals to counting calories. Nothing ever worked. It wasn't until I started studying which foods worked together in my Nutrition degree that I discovered that some foods actually work against each other, which in retrospect caused so many of my weight issues.

I know that looking (and feeling!) good is what a lot of women crave, which is why I've developed my Top 10 smoothie recipes for busy women who don't have time to eat healthily. They all have only 5 ingredients that you can buy in any supermarket."

SUMMARY

Customer and client interactions are a goldmine for finding out exactly how they describe their problems. Collect this information and use it for your own personal use in your offers and social media content. Tell stories and write longer posts to engage your clients more. The more you talk about the problems people are having, you'll then be able to position yourself as having the solution.

Take Action Now

If you speak to your potential customers on the phone...
- Write down how they describe the problem they're having and why they called you

If they fill out a questionnaire prior to their visit...
- How do they write about their problems?

If you're part of online or face-to-face groups where people are having the problem that you solve...
- Why do they ask questions in the group?

If there are books written about your particular topic with reviews on Amazon...
- Why do people say they read the book?
- Do they give them a favourable review? Why / why not?

Start to compile all this information. Use it as a reference for social media post ideas and for creating lead magnets.

Extend this further:

These techniques work incredibly well for Facebook and Instagram ad copywriting. I share all of this in my Adsolutely Fabulous Business Crew coaching program. If you'd like to join the waitlist for the next round visit https://mirandaivey.com/fabulous

CHAPTER 7

Actively Attract Leads

"Stop acting so small.
You are the universe in ecstatic motion."

- RUMI

When you grow a fanbase on social media, this can be a great way to help get your business 'out there'. However this fanbase is located on Facebook or Instagram, platforms you don't control and could shut down (or shut you out) tomorrow.

I've spoken to so many business owners over the years who lament that "overnight my reach dropped by thousands" or "I don't know what's happening on Instagram right now, but no one is seeing my posts." Building your email list is something you can control.

Sure, you're subject to inbox and deliverability issues (that Gmail Promotions folder is the bane of my existence!) but many top online entrepreneurs agree that building your email list and communicating regularly is still one of the top ways to grow your business and make money online.

START CREATING CONNECTION TODAY

When a potential customer is scrolling through social media, they're there for inspiration, lighthearted relief and to connect with family and friends. They're not always thinking about the problems they're having.

This where your lead magnet comes in. This is the middle step in the Path of Ascension that will see them take a leap from social media, visiting your website to 'sign up for something that will solve one of their problems.'

The thing is, your potential customers don't want to leave Facebook or Instagram. They're quite happy there. In order for them to make the leap over to your website and sign up, you need to give them a really good reason to do so.

There's no denying it, your customers are a savvy bunch. They're not going to leave Facebook without a good reason. They're definitely not going to give out their email addresses lightly. You need to be offering a solution to one of their problems.

WHICH TYPE OF LEAD MAGNET IS RIGHT FOR YOU?

In my own business, I sell a marketing and business coaching program. I educate people on the problems they might be having with attracting new clients to their business and feeling overwhelmed by social media marketing.

When I simply want to build brand awareness and grow my mailing list, a passive lead magnet works well. I then promote this using social media posts and paid ads. When I have a specific course start date in mine I need to turn people from a lead into a client faster. Therefore an active lead magnet is required.

PASSIVE LEAD MAGNETS

They're about the long(er) game. You're happy to be bringing in leads over time to build trust. These types of lead magnets may not always convert people into customers quickly but they will grow your email list and ability to market to a larger audience.

- Survey
- Ebook
- Cheat Sheet
- Guide
- Evergreen video series
- Evergreen webinar[4]

---

[4] Evergreen webinars use platforms such as *Easy Webinar or Webinar Jam* to offer set times for people to watch. The follow up emails can sometimes make people think they're watching something live. Evergreen webinars have lower attendance and conversion rates than live webinars.

ACTIVE LEAD MAGNETS

Active lead magnets are about fast-tracking your like, know, and trust factor. In order for people to consume your quality content, they need to commit with more than just their email address. They also have to show up at a particular time and sometimes even make a purchase as well. The difference is that you also need to commit time and energy as well.

- Live Webinar
- Live Challenge
- Free workshop or training
- Low cost workshop
- Discovery call

SOMEONE GIVES YOU THEIR EMAIL ADDRESS... THEN WHAT?

Your emails need to be collected into a database. Most entrepreneurs start out using MailChimp (mailchimp.com) as it's easy to set up and has a free basic version. There are many different options out there ranging in price depending on the level of complexity you require. Make sure you ask others so you're not paying for features you don't need. No matter which platform you use, when someone signs up to your lead magnet, do you have a strategy for what you're going to do with them next?

The usual response I hear from people is *'Oh yes, they sign up for my free recipe book, receive that, and then go onto my email list.'*

In order to build trust, you need to map out where you want them to go. This is usually with a series of emails. You might move them along to booking a call with you, purchasing a low-cost product or just providing information to them. You need to start to build trust that you'll show up like you said you would.

You're nurturing them (which is why it's often called a "nurture sequence"). More than anything, the goal of attracting leads and then regularly communicating with them is that they're going to get to know you. They will start to like you. Then they will trust that you have the solution they need.

CASE STUDY: HOW TO USE A LEAD MAGNET TO IDENTIFY A PROBLEM FOR YOUR CLIENTS

Jules Galloway is a Naturopath who works in women's health. Her specialty is adrenal fatigue, a condition that affects women, often mums, aged 35 - 55.

As it's the type of condition that the majority of women (and even some doctors) have never heard of, her online marketing needs to describe the condition and potentially the problems these women are having. She knows that her clients aren't googling 'adrenal fatigue' because they don't know what it is yet.

In order to move people up her Path of Ascension to book in for consultations, Jules came up with a free survey as her lead magnet.

Jules' Path of Ascension looks like this:

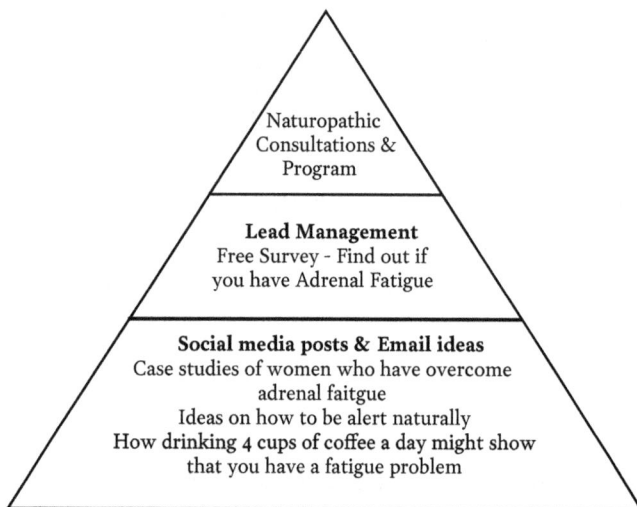

Naturopathic
Consultations &
Program

Lead Management
Free Survey - Find out if
you have Adrenal Fatigue

Social media posts & Email ideas
Case studies of women who have overcome
adrenal faitgue
Ideas on how to be alert naturally
How drinking 4 cups of coffee a day might show
that you have a fatigue problem

Using the Path of Ascension, Jules knows that it's hard to get people to go from one social media post to book in a consultation. On the other hand, she'll find it much easier to take them from a social media post to asking for their email address in return for assessing their risk of adrenal fatigue.

The other benefit of creating a lead magnet is that it puts you in a position of authority and people will *know* that you're the one to buy from. To build her leads, Jules has been running low cost Facebook ads for her free health check survey for almost two years. They have been consistently bringing in clients for her and building her authority in this area as well. See the health check for yourself at: https://julesgalloway.com/health-check/

SUMMARY

A lead magnet bridges the gap between your social media posts and what you want to sell. It's an opportunity for someone to make more of a commitment than a simple 'like' on a post. The right lead magnet will move your ideal customers up your Path of Ascension and closer to becoming a client.

Every online business needs a lead magnet to build their mailing list. Best of all, when you have a lead magnet you love you'll be so excited to share it everywhere!

Take Action Now

Everyone's lead magnet is different because everyone's business is different. Your lead magnet needs to solve a specific problem for your specific audience. You don't want to make more problems for your audience and confuse them. Nor do you want to try and solve all their problems so that they don't need you.
Brainstorm your lead magnet
- List 5 - 10 problems that your target audience currently have that relate to what you sell.
- List 5 - 10 desires that they would like to have in their life
- List 5 - 10 reasons why they wouldn't buy what you're selling

Use the templates below to come up with a winning lead magnet idea.

1. How they can overcome (one of their problems) to (reach their desire) without having to (reason why they won't buy)

Or

2. Why (one of your problems) is stopping you from (reaching desire) (then offer a solution)

Jules' example:

- Find out the symptoms of adrenal fatigue so you can enjoy more energy without drinking coffee all day
- Why eating sugary treats is actually stopping you from feeling better (and what you can do about it!)

In my own business:

- How to attract more customers to grow your business without it taking forever
- How to be visible online and attract more customers without giving them the hard sell or appearing sleazy
- How to grow your business with consistent lead generation and run a business that you love

CHAPTER 8

Build Trust By Showing Up

"We are what we repeatedly do.
Excellence then, is not an act, but a habit."

— ARISTOTLE

Using trust to build an online business is the long game. As fans, followers and email subscribers start to trust you, you'll be running a sustainable business into the future. In order to build this trust, you have to show up for them. All. The. Time.

When I speak with an entrepreneur about using a lead magnet to grow their email list, I always ask *'Once someone signs up, then what?* If the response is, *'I might email... maybe once a month? But I have been busy lately...'* I know that they're missing a vital trust building opportunity.

As a byproduct of showing up for others and putting some parameters for yourself, it's guaranteed creativity will flow.

If you consider yourself a friend who shows up when they said...

If you want to run an online business from anywhere...

If you want to build a fanbase of loyal customers...

Keep reading.

BE CONSISTENT (EVEN WHEN YOU DON'T WANT TO BE)

One of my favourite ways to create content is to take myself to my local cafe. If I'm feeling stuck or lacking ideas, I'll sit there with my laptop drinking my large coconut cappuccino and ask myself *"If I knew that this post could result in thousands of dollars by saying what I want to say, not what I think I should say, what would it be?'*

This can be incredibly liberating, especially if you're someone who gets stressed out over what to post and when.

The simplest way to start being an authority (and being comfortable sharing stories about yourself all the time) is by setting up a schedule to do so. The sooner you start with yourself, the sooner everyone else will know.

Consistency can simply be a commitment you make with yourself for example *'I'll do a Facebook live video every Wednesday at 12 pm.'* This works even better when you make a public commitment so that you feel obliged to show up (instead of coming up with 45 reasons not to do it on a Wednesday morning).

THERE'S SO MUCH CONTENT INSIDE YOU

When I suggest this to people they often worry that they'll run out of things to say. They believe that they'll give away so much free content that there will be nothing left to be paid for. However, by using the building authority content ideas from Chapter 4 what often happens is quite the opposite.

Once they hold themselves to task, they begin to burst with creativity. If you've been struggling with consistency this may be a great place to start.

There are many different ways you can hold yourself accountable to get your creative juices flowing. Just choose one thing to start with so that you don't become overwhelmed.

Some ideas are:

- Posting a weekly video on social media
- A weekly Facebook or Instagram Live
- Posting on Instagram on certain days of the week
- Sending out an email newsletter on a particular day every week

HOW OFTEN ARE YOU EMAILING YOUR LIST?

For years I'd been inconsistent with sending out my email newsletters to my database. Even though my 'list' had grown to several thousand subscribers, I told myself I was too busy to talk to them. Or I hid behind the excuse that I didn't know what to say or I didn't want to seem like I was 'spamming' them. I found it easier to simply ignore everyone.

This was fine until I wanted the people on my database to 'buy my stuff'. I'd send out a series of overly promotional emails, which came across as a grab for cash. Seeing as I hadn't shown up regularly, I had little rapport with my subscribers and they barely knew me, let alone trusted me. I certainly didn't come across as the go-to person who will solve their online marketing problems.

Since the start of 2019, I've made it my creative mission to email every Thursday morning. I write and send out an email whether I'm selling something or not . The feedback I've received shows that my email content is connecting with people. The goal has simply been to build trust.

Writing an email every week may seem time consuming. That's why you can use the repurposing techniques from Chapter 5. You'll find that weekly emails take less and less time. Despite only working part-time with young kids for several years, whenever I bump into someone who is on my mailing list in person they say to me, *you seem to be everywhere!*

Regardless of whether your email list is in the tens, the hundreds or the tens of thousands, the time is now to value and nurture every single human that is on your list.

SHOW UP FOR YOURSELF

I guarantee magic happens in your business with regular email communication to your list. There is power in regularly writing and sharing about what you're doing. You'll become visible here, there and everywhere. Then when it's time to launch your new product, service or program, you'll now have a ready-made audience of people who you've built a relationship with over time.

I understand that emailing your list can seem like a drag because it can feel like another thing on a never ending to-do list. However, it's also an opportunity to be in front of a group of people who have already SHOWN AN INTEREST IN YOUR BUSINESS.

If your database includes current and former clients, these people THE MOST IMPORTANT people (aside from you!) in your business. Over time, you'll find the same people come back time and time again for your services as you have built trust with them. Surely they deserve (and want) to hear from you regularly?

SUMMARY

For any online business, email marketing needs to underpin your social media or paid advertising strategy. There's no point spending time and money on driving traffic to your website or 'building your list' if you don't regularly email your list.

Take Action Now:

- When was the last time you emailed your list?
- If your answer makes you feel queasy it's time to change this today
- Is there a social post or video that went well for you recently? As in, people liked, commented or shared it?
- Use the repurposing techniques from Chapter 5 to spark inspiration for your next newsletter
- Choose one type of marketing that you will consistently use weekly. Make it non-negotiable that this gets done every week, even if you end up posting at 9pm on Friday night
- Being consistent becomes easier over time, the key is to start today!
- When you're ready to get 'out there' even more consistently, join the waitlist for my Adsolutely Fabulous Business Crew at https://mirandaivey. com/fabulous

CHAPTER 9

Don't Just Ask Once, Ask Twice. And Then Maybe A Few More Times.

"He who is ashamed of asking is afraid of learning"

- DANISH PROVERB

When it comes to selling online, chances are people didn't see your Facebook post the first time. Maybe they missed your Instagram story (they disappear after 24 hrs so they probably did). They may not have read your email. This means they haven't heard about the 'thing' that you're selling.

This is why creating a strategy of showing up online frequently will be the secret to your success. If you've ever found that people didn't buy from you straight away, have your moment of sadness and then move on. This one failure may be one of the best things to happen to your business.

As in the proverb above, if you hadn't tried to sell people your "stuff", then you wouldn't have learned anything about what your customers want. Marketing and selling is a never-ending quest to put your products and services in front of the right group of people at the right time.

Want to know another secret? Planning can get your ideas out of your head so you can start to be creative and enjoy yourself!

GET OUT OF YOUR OWN HEAD

By now you have some excellent ideas for content that connects with your customers. This is the type of content that positions you as an authority. You know what problem you solve, how you solve it and who you solve it for. You know that you need to email your database regularly in order to build trust.

All of your grand ideas to take over your industry (or the world), all of those products you're going to sell, all of the amazing online courses you're going to create... Let's make these ideas into reality.

The best way to turn ideas into real life? Create a Marketing Calendar.

MAKE YOUR TASKS MANAGEABLE

Here's the full Mark Twain quote from Chapter 1:

"The secret of getting ahead is getting started. The secret of getting started is breaking your complex overwhelming tasks into manageable tasks, and then starting on the first one."

Many people have told me that they consider Marketing Calendars to be boring, hard work and unachievable. I challenge you to think of them as a treasure map for people to start finding out about what you do and sell.

By reading this book you now know *where* you want to take people using the Path of Ascension and *what* type of marketing content to create. By getting all of these ideas out of your head and onto paper, a Marketing Calendar is *how* you're going to get there.

Step 1 - Set up your Marketing Calendar

Find a Calendar style that works for you. My preferred method for starting a calendar is printing out an A4 sized monthly calendar and writing down my plan using a pen and paper.

If you want to use Google Sheets or an excel spreadsheet, you can edit these on your computer. You can download examples of both at https://mirandaivey.com/calendar.

Some people like using Trello (trello.com), an online program that acts like virtual post-it notes that can be easily moved. Whatever you think will be a system that you will enjoy and remember to use, go for that.

I suggest planning at least two weeks to one month in advance. If you know you have multiple events, special launches or products becoming available, plan over several months. I wouldn't suggest going any further into the future (although you can!) as it's important that your marketing feels light to be accomplished.

Step 2 - Start with your life non-negotiables

Once you've got your calendar printed, or on your computer it's time to get cracking! Add in your own life events such as holidays, work commitments, family events, sports, weekly fitness sessions and appointments. This is the first step to making your marketing work. It won't if it clashes with everything else that goes on in your life.

Add in school holidays if you're a working parent. I've been on the marketing team for entrepreneurs who have launched online programs coinciding with the start of the school year. As parents first and entrepreneurs second, their children required extra attention, then their marketing efforts and posting on social media fell by the wayside. This meant that their sales weren't as high as expected.

Note: You don't need to post on social media every day however if you're in a promotional period for a new product, service or program you'll want to make sure that your attention isn't being split 17 ways.

Finally, add in other special days such as Christmas, Mother's Day, end of Financial Year and the online shopping event Black Friday / Cyber Monday (held over Thanksgiving weekend in the United States). If these days have an impact on your audience and could provide you with ideas for content to link with your promotions, they're great for planning ahead.

Of course, there's always unprecedented events (a pandemic comes to mind...) but if you do life first then focus on online marketing second, you'll find yourself less stressed.

Step 3 - Create marketing momentum

Every month in your marketing calendar needs momentum, a purpose that underpins how you're moving people up the Path of Ascension. Your ultimate goal may be in three months but starting now will see you achieve what you're aiming for. Write this at the top of your calendar.

Some examples of monthly marketing momentum:

- Building your email list and so you'll make sure that you're promoting opportunities to sign up to your mailing list during the month
- Promoting a special event or workshop. You need to mention it on your social media several times, send emails and create multiple touch points to ensure that everyone knows to 'buy a ticket'
- Featuring a particular aspect of what you do for the month - e.g. for a Naturopath, it could be gut health, or for a Physiotherapist, it may be knee injuries. No one else needs to know, but putting this onto paper will give you ideas for content creation
- A special offer, bundle of products or timely promotions based on other events such as Mothers Day or Christmas

By now you've learnt that most people won't go straight from one Facebook post to purchasing your product or service. Therefore the point of your monthly marketing calendar is to build hype and momentum over time.

Step 4 - Add your linchpin

In Chapter 6, I discussed finding your own marketing linchpin. That one type of promotion that you will do every week without fail. I started with a weekly short video uploaded to Facebook. I then used this as the basis for my weekly emails to my email database.

Choose a way of marketing that you enjoy doing that you find easy to do. There's no point beating yourself up every week for not doing a 20 minute free online training video because you don't even enjoy making videos.

Add the day and time that this will be published every week. Remember how we added your life non-negotiables first? If you know that you love going to the gym every Thursday morning, it wouldn't make sense to send out your weekly email on Thursday mornings. Trying to do two things at once will see one of them lose and I'll bet it will usually be your marketing.

After you've added in your linchpin every week, plan out ideas for the rest of your social content. Focus on only sharing one idea per week and repurposing it across multiple platforms. This will save you time when it comes to coming up with new content ideas.

If you are going to be promoting a particular product or service, how many different angles or ways can you start talking about it? Start brainstorming!

Remember this is a process that you will repeat again and again. The first time you create a marketing calendar, it will seem like hard work and may take longer than you thought.

HOW TO RUN AN ONLINE PROGRAM LAUNCH

If you're working towards an online program launch, rather than simply telling everyone your program is available, it's a good idea to use a live lead event such as a webinar, 5-day challenge or workshop to build hype.

These types of events are great for creating momentum and giving people the opportunity to find out more. This is the type of event that you can promote using paid Facebook and Instagram ads.

Once you've held your event, you then have what's called a Cart Open period. This is approximately a week where you promote the program on your social media and email marketing before you start the program.

Add to your Marketing Calendar:
- Pre-promotion for Live Webinar: 7 May - 20 May (market via Facebook and Instagram social posts, emails, videos, paid social media ads)
- Live Webinar: 21 May
- Cart Open: 21 May - 27 May (market via Facebook and Instagram social posts, emails, videos, paid social media ads)
- Course Starts: 28 May

I've written a guide for online program launches called 28 Days to Launch available at: https://www.adsolutelyfabulous.com/28-days-launch

SUMMARY

Most people fail to sell their stuff not because their stuff is poor quality but usually because they've failed to be comfortable in talking about it over and over again. By creating your own marketing calendar that suits your life it will no longer be shoved to the back of your to-do list. Start with your "linchpin" as a weekly commitment and build your marketing momentum from there.

Take Action Now:

- Step 1 - Set up your marketing calendar. Download an example from https://mirandaivey.com/calendar
- Step 2 - Add in your life non-negotiables
- Step 3 - Write down your monthly marketing purpose
- Step 4 - Commit to a weekly marketing linchpin. Then brainstorm ideas to weave in stories about why people really need to buy your stuff!
- Monthly reflection - At the start of each month make a time to plan out the upcoming weeks. Conduct a review of your previous month. How many of your promotions did you remember to do?

PEOPLE DO WANT TO BUY YOUR STUFF

The time is now to overcome your fear of marketing or promoting ourselves online. The fear that we have to look perfect before we're allowed to be visible online. The fear that if we put out our own opinions people won't like us. The fear that emailing our database will see our subscriber numbers go down.

But there's another fear at play. My fear is that if you don't put yourself out there being who you truly are and then your potential customers won't know that you exist. They'll miss out on the important ways you can help them live happier, healthier, better lives.

I wrote this book to help you overcome your fears. To realise that there is value in being different and there is a bucketload of value in standing for something. Your voice matters. It's time to stop hiding. It's time to put yourself out there. There's so much more to gain.

There's people out there who do want to buy your stuff. Focus on how you want them to feel after they do business with you. It's not about what you're selling but why you're selling it. You're their shining light. The more that you hide because selling seems wrong, or that it's hard work, your people won't change at all.

Your job now is to be 100% aligned with your message. Your primary role is to share your uniqueness with the world. You have moved on from 'if I build a website, they will come'. Your mantra is now, 'If I turn up every day and share my unique message with the world, moving people towards my ultimate goal, then they will come.'

I love that you've taken the leap to run an online business and I want you to know that I see you and I feel you. I want to hear you. Go forth and spread your message. Your people are waiting to buy from you.

Stay fabulous.

ACKNOWLEDGMENTS

I'd like to thank everyone who said they would be excited to read my book. It was putting this idea out into the world that saw me keep going. Yvette and Angela, without either of you there would be no businesses and no book. Sammy for being my proofreader and Tom for your final edits. Emma, your course gave this book the structure it desperately needed. Victoria, Hayley, Katie you all were in my corner. Mum, you never gave up believing you would one day read my book. Dad, I wrote this because you never did.

ABOUT MIRANDA IVEY

In *No One Wants to Buy Your Stuff* Miranda Ivey leans on over 15 years experience in marketing and PR. Having helped sell everything from artistic performances to meditation memberships and a hundred other types of businesses in between, she loves helping people tap into the power of their own story

Find her online: mirandaivey.com